LOOK, CLARE! LOOK!

Clare Pollard was born in 1978 in Bolton. After studying at Cambridge she moved to London, where she now lives. She has published three collections of poetry with Bloodaxe: *The Heavy-Petting Zoo* (1998), which she wrote whilst still at school; *Bedtime* (2002); and *Look, Clare! Look!* (2005). Her first play *The Weather* (Faber, 2004) premièred at *The Royal Court Theatre*.

Clare has supported her writing with jobs as a cinema usher, a barmaid, Managing Editor of *The Idler* magazine and assistant director of the Clerkenwell Literary Festival. She is currently editing the poetry journal *Reactions*.

CLARE POLLARD

Look, Clare!
Look!

*To Angela
Best
Pollard x*

BLOODAXE BOOKS

ISBN: 1 85224 709 6

First published 2005 by
Bloodaxe Books Ltd,
Highgreen,
Tarset,
Northumberland NE48 1RP.

www.bloodaxebooks.com
For further information about Bloodaxe titles
please visit our website or write to
the above address for a catalogue.

Bloodaxe Books Ltd acknowledges
the financial assistance of
Arts Council England, North East.

Cover printing by J. Thomson Colour Printers Ltd, Glasgow.

Printed in Great Britain by
Bell & Bain Limited, Glasgow, Scotland.

For my father,
who gave me my love of travel,
and my love of home.

ACKNOWLEDGEMENTS

Acknowledgements are due to the editors of the following publications where some of these poems first appeared: *Converging Lines* (British Council, 2004), *Magma*, *Rising*, *Ootal* (Sweden), *Rising* and www.thepoem.co.uk.

I would also like to thank Arts Council England for a writer's award, the Society of Authors for a travel grant, and my husband (and muse) Richard Henson for the map.

CONTENTS

THE MUSE

THE JOURN

THE POET

Other animals do not need a purpose in life. A contradiction to itself, the human animal cannot do without one. Can we not think of the aim of life as being simply to see?

JOHN GRAY,
Straw Dogs

I

The Journey

The Journey

You say Big Mac
We say fight back
> Cry at anti-globalisation march,
> MAYDAY 2002

China

Dumplings were sold on every cluttered corner –
their dour, pinched faces sweating in bamboo stacks – *personification*
that cost 10Y or so, nothing to us.

There were bluish pines blurry with snow, *theatre*
and other trees, like calligraphy,
and trees operatic with caged birds
twitchy and puppetted behind their coloured masks.

There was a zoo, too, stumbled on by accident – *poverty*
a joke at first, the poor show of those threadbare camels, *cruelty*
but then that poor bear banging bar to skull,
kids pelting it with litter, a cheese-tease on a stick.
And the tiger's boxed pace – two steps, two steps –
its shrunken mewl.

Strange to see such beauty, such life – muscle and blood –
turned grotesque by our crazed rush to turn the whole world *safe*,
like the Starbucks, with its regulation cups, that surprised us
beneath the Forbidden City's gold glazed tiles.

And those two fathers – Colonel Sanders, Chairman Mao – *contrast*
gazed out on every scene with twin bland smiles,
watched over each end of Tiananmen Square, *meaningless*
that vacancy, vast, like memory loss.

The guy in the park said: *Mao was a great man,* *hidden*
but there were things done, of which no one speaks: *meaning*
pigs that troughed and shat in mosques, *+ history*
libraries torched, teachers beaten dumb by students,
so many friends betrayed by their friends.

13

We bought a watch where Mao's arm moves when it ticks:
complicit in how time turns evil into kitsch.

I heard of other evils too:
of thousands killed to keep the secret of squander –
a terracotta army in the earth –
and of how little this mattered.
Of students mown down screaming for fairness.
A traveller's throat slit for his moneybelt.

[handwritten margin note: violence / savagery / helplessness]

I saw skies so full of filth the stars were all put out,
and bags dip and fly across the flat, farmed fields
in their thousands – a plague of doves –

and thought: with all this harm done
can it really come all right in the end?

Bangkok

In sweat-dark night,
in eye-burn light,
they rack up fake T-shirts
and holler: 'razor minge'
'rainbow pussy'
'ping pong banana'.

[handwritten margin note: discomfort]

[handwritten margin note: Sexual imagery / Sex sells]

Girls in tangerine bikinis –
the prettiest by the doors –
indifferently whore,
clinging to poles,
slick dark Asian cunt imaginable,
snail-wet beneath the slice of thong.

And you can flash a light
from the velveteen dark,
and she'll descend –
shy-smiling, costly angel –
and fumble your bad, *bad* cock
beneath the cocktail sticky table,

[handwritten margin note: light / dark]

14

younger than your youngest daughter,   *shock*
or perhaps your first fuck –
you don't ask if she likes movies,
or reads poetry,
or thinks this is bad luck,
or why her cheeks feel papaya-damp.

Ladyboys shriek like parrots,
whilst women line up in best gowns –
as though for graduation –
in that clinging fried pong of meat;
in razor night,   *repetition first stanza*
in rainbow light.

Cambodia

begins with a positive

And yet hope exists, despite everything,
in stilted shacks, amongst a fatherless people.
We arrived to a night lit by sheets of electric,
and acres of dust,
and chicks and piebald pigs scrubbing round palms,
and giddy girls balancing trays of locusts at loo-stops,   *poverty*
eyes scrunched to the glare of our wealth.

At Angkor, trees coupled and wrestled with stone –   *mish mash*
jungle pulping indifferent faces, growths bursting   *deformity*
through the bellies of elephants, whilst we relished   *wrongness*
the brutalised beauty;
those tragic, fallen things.
Children chanted: *dollar, dollar,*
a limbless boy begged amongst the ruins.

In Phnom Penh sun set as we spooned curry down.
There was a free pool table,
a joint passed around.
Davvy had sequined sandals and two dead parents
and danced, fingers twisting to gorgeous deformities,
and picked up backpackers – $20 a go.
She laughed a lot.
Bats flapped over the lake.

15

In Phnom Penh men loll outside the guesthouses all day,
skins golden and opulent with dust, lighting cigarettes,
motorbikes inert between their muscled thighs.
They wait for us.
They wait for tipsy girls and sunburnt boys
to mount their bikes – cameras ready, wallets fat with luck –
and say *go here*, *go there*,
and never question what might happen
if they took us somewhere else,
if they just drove somewhere else.

At the shooting range the AK-47 made you look
so young – thirteen or something –
with its awkward rest against your chest,
the violence of its kick: *bang bang*,
the love-bites it left on your shoulder.
And did you see those photos on the wall – other tourists
baring their teeth like 'Nam-movie vets,
grotesque?

And then the killing fields.

Contrast

It is hard, in the space of the field,
its small, dug plots, its sane green,
to picture thousands herded towards pits
for reading, for wearing glasses, for cousins
or grandchildren deemed to be guilty.

It is difficult, faced with the pile of scraps
to picture each dress or shirt whole:
hand-me-down or sewn by a grandma,
selected, perhaps, for red petals in the print.
Stained with melon juice, frayed, neat.

poignant
heartbreaking

It is hard, in the small space of time,
to do each skull the dignity of picturing
a soft fur of hair over the pearl bone,
eyes in sockets, lips cushioning the teeth.
Hated, heavy brows, or a small scar.

Vietnam

Saigon was a child at the front of a Honda,
her dad behind, then her mum clutching on –
that limpet-shell hat, that outfit, like floral pyjamas –
as they roared round a turquoise corner
into the narrow peach and workwear blue,
the smell of mint leaves and boiled beef bone.
A dog's bark. A crouched woman's shadow.

The guy on the coach said: *we didn't hate the GIs.*
They were just kids, how could we hate them?
You should have seen them weep when the helicopters came
at leaving; for what they left.

youth
ignorance

But I have seen the traps they left for those children –
sea-urchins of steel, or bamboo beast-pits
spiked with cobra poison for a slow death.
And I have seen what those kids did too:
foetuses lemur-eyed, bulging, bent as a dancers' fingers.
Acres of forest and flesh burnt dead.

And we were just kids too,
all catching the same buses up the same coast,
necking the same cocktails by the same sand with the same itinerary:
tunnels – lobster – Hoi An – the mausoleums.

We met a man who earned $17 a week,
and asked us what we earned,
and we felt obscene,
were obscene:
the casual flamboyance with which we bought a Coke, say, or Pringles.

We are the same age as those GIs.
ignorance
carelessness

17

Laos

To get to Thailand, we drove back through Laos.
The infrastructure there is very poor.
Apparently, it's due to nine long years
during which the US waged secret war.

I wonder why they thought news of the scare
they gave the commie scum could not be shared?
One more exotic place name bombed to shit.
It's generous, to guess we would have cared.

Thailand II   DEBAUCHERY

Back in Thailand, we met mates in Khao San –   Silliness
beside the bar's blare of pirate movies,   youth
banana pancakes, shakes,   reckless
gap year girls getting fake tattoos and ratty braids
because it's an *experience* –
and got slaughtered on buckets of samsong, Coke and Red Bull,
sucking ourselves silly through their clutches of straws.
We danced, fell over, can't remember, really.
I had a handbag stolen, a camera.
All sense of joy.

Puking outside the police station next morning,
I wept with anger because some stranger
did not think that I deserved to keep things.

Down to the coast. A bus. Ferries.
We partied on beaches lit by paraffin lamps,
listening to tunes whilst hippies juggled flames.
It whirled in wheels;
the moon fattened.

There were diet pills – pink ones and blues.
Matt ran through fire and fell and blistered his hand,
and I thought: it must have been this crowd in Bali.

Then the full moon came, party boats speeding in.
Neon flags burnt in the gut-melting bass,
and tourists bought 'buckets of joy' and doughnuts,   *irony*
and there were tiny blue jellyfish punctuating the bay –
violets pressed flat between pages –
where the men lined up to piss, as though at a huge urinal,

and soon it was a heave of flesh,   *body imagery*
and the piss got lapped back,
and a Thai boy searched for his mother,
and mashed men slipped to slumber like the corpses of beached whales,
and others stumbled somehow into pissy shallows,
and had to be saved.

I remember how that night the sky was huge and clean
but we were a fucking mess: *debauchery*
                                                      decay
you wanted us to watch the sunrise together,   *dissolute*
but I was too drunk to be bothered,
and you slashed your foot open on a broken bottle
running up the sands to find me,
                              and bled so hard.

The next day we fled the island –
sand lumpen with fag ends, straws, johnny wrappers,   *unpleasant*
the scum on the sea,
the taste in the mouth –
for another with pale green tortoiseshell water
and coral flickering with rainbow fish,
and parts turned to death by the nudge of a fin or a foot.

The man in the bar asked: *why do you hate Iraq?*
as the hulking ships closed in on CNN,
as the dusty camps set up,
as the choppers descended,
and we tried to explain over beers or Mai Tais
that we didn't, we hated the war.

That there was just nothing we could do.

Burma (Interlude)

COMPLACENCE

We went on a day trip to Myanmar
and gave the Burmese military our baht
contributing to the oppression there.
I can't say that I took it much to heart –

*apathy
ignorance
complacence*

as the sea-eagles swooned over our boat
I was too keen to see and hear and smell
that world which nestled in the swelling hills
(and yeah, get my visa renewed as well.)

I wandered round the port. The men wore skirts.
I drank a strong, sweet coffee, passed the time.
The Buddha watched me idly from above
her golden smile as complacent as mine.

tired

Thailand III

ALIEN

Back in Thailand, we ventured into forests
where hilltribes in turbans and bright, woven skirts –
with bell-clanking cattle, slender-nosed elephants,
cockerels that woke us at 4.00 a.m. –
smoked beside their raised huts, and let us gawp,
and our guide gave us sandwiches and nothing spicy
in case our delicate stomachs could not stomach it.

clumsy?

alien

The hills were ruffled with smoke in the morning,
because it was April, when they loosed fire to tear through their fields,
and a girl on the slope of the river caught a net of cicadas
to scoff, like whirring, juicy crisps.

contrast lifestyles

We first learnt of SARs there, from another backpacker,
nervous about cancelled flights; quarantine.
We learnt we were carriers, those of us who travelled:
jetting from place to place with our cargo of death,
bringing panic in beads on our breath,
turning cities to ghost towns,

and apparently the war was getting dull.

In our last weeks we met such creatures:
bulging-eyed bullfrogs that bellowed hellos,
puffer fishes that puffed up like torture weapons,
fiddler crabs that waved one freakishly fat claw,   *alien*
slender lime pythons that *hsssssssssssssss*-ed,
giant tortoises that slobbered bugs off cracked lips,
a slow loris, that goggled through cartoon eyes,
fireflies that made Christmas trees of jungle...

But no sought-after gibbons –   *metaphor*
they flee from humans,
remembering slaughter and stolen children and no good.

Singapore Airport

Changed planes at Singapore
and before you start to ask –
yes, it has a swimming pool,
no, I didn't wear a mask.

FAMILIAR

Australia (South Coast and the Centre)   *Contrast to Asia*

At first there's relief in the wealth of it.
Civilisation.   *Superiority*
To go into a supermarket, for example, with rows of fridges
bright as a movie-star's teeth, eight types of dip,
and a brand of wine that you know is reliably quaffable.   *the 'known'*
The flawless drive down the Great Ocean Road –
like a real-life car commercial –
to the vineyards, their autumn colours of pumpkin and brass.
But then the safeness falters.   *beauty / safe*
Perhaps on the step outside the liquor store –
where shadows hunch in the sun's bleach, slurping tawny port –
or when the bus drives into redness and keeps on driving,
past roadkill that trembles with flies and riverbeds licked dry,
and you could die out there and the birds would tug off your flesh
and the spiders lace your bones together.

there's still misery + danger

21

Amongst our favourite things in Australia are the Big Things,
which are just these huge, huge things, basically,
like a Big Rocking Horse, say,
or a Big Mango,
and are so touchingly human and pointless yet somehow impressive,
and the first that we pass is a sheep,
but then there's other Big Things in the centre –
no longer man's attempts, but *real* things, nature.
Knuckles of rock as monstrous as god –
vast bent-backed, plague-pocked stones,   *ageless*
bloodied by babes left out for eagles.

The man in the hostel says: *they complain*
but there's more of them now than when we landed.
                                        racism

                We belong to this country
                We look after this country

And our tour guide declares: *any questions in your life*
you can find out the answers at Uluru,
but we don't, of course.
Lightning cuts the bruised sky.
There are complaints in our group that the tour does not provide
enough cheese for vegetarians at lunch.

The news is: *the war in Iraq is as good as won,*
and: *a ship full of asylum seekers is thought to be heading towards us,*
and: *today in court the Bali bomber smiled.*

The dog-proof fence keeps beasts back.
Drought is crippling the farmers.

The dog-proof fence keeps beasts back.   *repetition*

                        immigration
                            'them' and 'us'

Australia (East Coast)

Everything's easy on the east coast.
Everything's packaged and organised.
FREE meals with your dorm, at bars
with $6 jugs, wet t-shirts, GUARANTEED laughs,   *empty*

22

and every drive's a Scenic Tourist Drive,
and every walk's a Tourist Nature Boardwalk
with helpful pictures of the earth's crust, whales etc.

[handwritten: packaged, promoted, perfect, unreal]

And nothing seems real to me.

Everything's easy on the east coast.
If you waiver all insurance claims
the reef can be accessed on a FUN white boat
with FREE tropical smorgasbord lunch,
FREE snorkel, FREE fins, FREE trial dive,
and my hostel is offering FREE sheets,
which certainly sounds good value

[handwritten: repetition emphasises irony]

but nothing seems real to me.

It's been getting worse lately.
It's these tourist sights –
they've been removed from history.

[handwritten: Scathing, Sad, angry]

All those thousands of years of shifting plates,
of painstaking evolution of a skink or sooty gull,
all those layers of lives, those deaths, that power,
all those attempts at beauty…

And this is their point:
for kids to say: 'That's awesome, man' –
kids who've crossed a world to find *themselves*.
I pose by a shipwreck; you ask me to smile.

Fifteen minutes here, guys, then back to the bus.

New Zealand *[handwritten: NATURE]*

And when man first ran his canoe aground –
clutching weapons, the lean rat slinking out by his foot –
fur seals gawping through the soft clots of their eyes,
he must have been quick to realise

[handwritten: animals, nature]

that this land belonged to the birds,
the sky shivering with cormorant wings,
the tree-ferns loaded with shags,
the rocks frisking with amber-eyed penguins,

and beyond that, in rimu forest,
or above farting mud,
or circling the ashy lip of a volcano,
or dangling in the scent of a palm-lily,

kiwi, kea, moa, weka, kaka,
sooty shearwaters, bellbirds, black stilt,
fantails, falcons and tiny riflemans –
spiralling like dropped blue petals –

and the noise of it all at dawn!
It must have seemed that all hell cried out
in the nest of his skull,
and every voice in heaven,

and they must have flown to him,
not knowing –
the moreporks crying 'morepork'
and the whios crying 'whio' –

have flown not knowing to this strange tree,
to the scentless fruit of its hands
that would bring soon enough
the knowledge that this tree was death.

Fiji

Fiji was a walk beneath breadfruit trees,
papaya's heavy baubles,
to a shoreline rattling with chalky white bones of coral.
I would pick a spot, then unfurl my sarong like a flag,
read Updike or Pilger or lie
watching a boy playing touch rugby;
his mother in her prim floral dress – ankle to throat –
shy of the sun's slackening eye.

In evening dark winds banged the beach.
Village elders strummed child-sized guitars,
legs lean beneath grass skirts they wore for us.
I was offered a coconut shell of kava, and –
wanting to feel stoned –
bumped my lips to the donkey-rough skull.

> They would cut off a man's penis and make him gag on it.
> They would sup from the broken head of a man.

And on Sunday I dragged you to that neat white church –
over sand pocked with holes that hid
the tender nightmare bodies of crabs.
The children were so restless, suited and ribboned,
eyes resting on the window: its square of palm and blue –
but we saved them, I suppose,
we brought goodness, I suppose
(though at what cost?
With what truths lost?
With what doors slam-shutting around them?).
For dinner we had fish, just caught.
Sun bled behind the island's gothic set.

[handwritten annotations: "trying to understand", "Sadness", "missionaries", "GREED", "cynical consumerism"]

The Flight to America

I got the sleeper plane into LA,
except I found I couldn't sleep at all
as all the US kids were pretty hyped
and angry they'd been served a meal so small.

I'm going to America, I thought.
I have to say, it felt almost not right –
lately it had seemed America
was just something the world dreamt in the night.

America

Congested

Burgers were sold on every SUV-choked corner –
sat greasy and obese in processed buns –
that cost $1, all we could afford.

Westernised
consumerism

In LA's sprawl of boulevards, strung between skinny palms, Contrast
and sunsets the grimy apricot of fake tan,   the
and tramps who perform to invisible casting directors,   people
and prostitutes who dream of fictional characters
letting them loose with a gold Amex on Rodeo Drive,
there were alternatives: real and unreal
Pollo Loco, for example,
Taco Bell,
Jack-in-the-Box (for Philly cheesesteaks),
Subway (for subs),

insatiable
greed
hunger

? but mainly it was burgers,
heart-muting and salivating all over themselves.

And pulling out of the Greyhound station on the 3rd of July,
after 4 hours of queuing in a clatter of Spanish and babies –
with only 99c chicken nuggets for entertainment,
made of skin, apparently, that's why they're so juicy, ugh
with the drunks, the singers, the liars, the broke,
the old, bald lady who whispered vicious nonsense to herself –
a woman on the coach said: *I have to get out of this city.*
The people are cockroaches they won't leave me alone.
The people are cockroaches.

Don't get me wrong, I love America –   switcharound
the pop-art of cacti,   positive
the condors cutting through a canyon so huge, so red,
that your heart has to expand to meet it.
The unexpected poetry of that main street:
Wedding Dresses, Gun Shop, Psychic,   surreal
                                               exciting

and Americans too: Elvis, Billie, Anne,
all the novelists, poets, actors, civil rights leaders
and beautiful wasted waitresses in dead-end diners,
and we just *loved* Las Vegas,
the absurd, stupendous, gorgeous follies,

HUGE

the Grand Canal on the second floor, for god's sake,   *OTT*
and putting too much on red with a cheap margarita
and the heat, the *huge* heat, then a graveyard breakfast in Vegas,
and fucking on our huge, huge bed in *Vegas*,
and the strip like a sweetshop of neon,

but in our circus-themed hotel, beneath the leering, creepy clowns,
the graceless acrobats, the merry-go-round bar,   *desperate*
parents were feeding college funds to slots,
and people were feeding on all-they-could-eat, which was lots:
steak, pizza, pasta, prime rib, home fries, fried chicken, chilli cheese
        nachos, extra multi-mega large sodas,
and these aren't even the rich, ladies and gentlemen,
these people buying Vegas caps and cups, the tat with tits,
making room for the ice cream sprinkles pecan pie pudding extra slice,
laying another on 1, it's my lucky number,
ploughing in buckets and buckets of cents,   *excess*
all of us basking in the glut, the gluttony, the gold, the:
clink clink clink clink.

And I heard of Native Americans living in filth in trailers
and the Grand Canyon shimmering sometimes in a haze of filth,
as though on a bad TV set.

And whilst others struggled and sheltered in fear in Iraq,   *patriotism*
I saw caps declare 'American and Proud',
and red, white and blue pancakes you could 'eat with pride',
and red, white and blue watches so you could 'make time for your
        country',
and they were selling toy American soldiers –
they scrambled on their bellies down Venice Beach,
and their bellies said MADE IN CHINA.   *IRONY*

and I ordered a sandwich and there was literally, like, 2 inches of
        pastrami.

Who needs that much pastrami?   *INCREDULOUS*
                        Greed OTT

27

Mission Beach *shedding*

freedom
shedding

The hotel sat wild upon the hill,
amongst snakes dripping, paint, down the strangler figs.
We awoke to the croaks of purse-jawed frogs,
then breakfast in the green glow of fan-palms:
coffee, sun-split yoghurt, an ocean's wink.
Cassowaries, those boneheads, those prehistoric freaks,
padded amongst our rooms, creaky as puppets,
attacking the tourists – fierce despite their fewness –
striding boldly out before the bulb-eyed beasts
of four-wheel-drives.
The beach was perfect: just us.
I began to strip, all elbows and daring, and my breasts
flopped out, slightly silly and as blinding as the sand.
My nipples were that pink inside conch shells.
How we rushed into the splash, shedding everything!
We fell nude into the brilliant, cool, illuminated sea
and I have never been so happy.
My body could feel itself.
The wine tapped like adrenaline in my brow, and you,
you were slippery as a dolphin in my arms...
My love,
we didn't know that it was stinger season –
that my breasts might have been whipped raw,   *danger*
that your beautiful hairy chest might have floated
bang into a jellied sack of pain.
That you might have had to piss on me.   *reality*
That your heart could have stopped.
I have never been so happy.
I jumped and wrestled with you,
all the while thinking *thankyou, thankyou* –
though I didn't believe in god,
only those ancient blue-black birds
quietly loping in the forest above us.

II

The World and I

To Hua Shan

Birds thread above the sky-wept streams,
the sharp-toothed pines and snowy seams
and marks left here as pilgrims passed –
the coloured flags, the ribbons asked
for not by trees but by our hearts
that envy peace and want a part.

Though I'm light-drained
                  and hunger breath –
(blots of dark float:
               thumb tiny deaths
on my eyeballs,
          and lungs won't fill)
I will not go from here until
I've stood upon your northern peak
beside the monastery, too weak
to really take the landscape in –
what is it that I think I'll win?
Why do we call this holiness?
What do I think I will impress?
This jagged point of buckled rock?
The saffron monks?

               The freezing shock
of iced air skins my throat inside.
On this stone slope I cannot hide
my base desire to reach the top –
just like China itself can't drop
its need to steep Mao's name in praise:
no, communism can't erase
our love of power and dizzy heights –
although we know the climb's not right
and makes us sick – we save our face
careless of billions at the base.

30

To a Cambodian Sky

I'm in the street –
amongst beer girls, cyclos,
internet cafes –
with my head back, wondering
how those white eyes
that spray your hot blue,
could have looked down on the S21
and not shut them.

Then I remember that your stars
are dinosaur old.
They probably shut
and we just don't know,
and I am boozing and laughing
in the vest-top
that I've splattered with amok dt'ray
on the lip of an infinite dark.

To Mangos

[handwritten: erotic]

O fruit as erogenous zone! Blush mangos *[handwritten: excitement]*
hanging heady from these Vietnamese trees –
you're as exotic as paddy fields or cheongsams,
as the schoolgirls who laugh by the canals
where you drop and split: the skulls
of girls raped on these banks like animals *[handwritten: Shock ending]*

[handwritten: Sexuality]

To a Bonobo

O nimble-fingered Bonobo,
brother squatting in your soft coat,
can you at least understand us?
There are only words and fire between us.
Can you forgive us, for such diminishing?
Are we not all born greedy to seize?

empathy

Stop banging that manly brow,
stop screwing your – ew – your mother,
stop pooping dung they will shovel and bag,
your mouth a halved-coconut screeching *god god*
in some tribal tongue:
O please brother you're babbling!

humour

repulsion

To a Dartmoor Pony

Comes the time when all you rarities will graze
with unicorns in darker fields.

I would promise that meant no forgetting,
but soon we will forget even ourselves.

Sad

To Depression

(handwritten: resignation wry humour)

So good morning,
you're back,
and I make up black coffee like you've never been away,
whilst – shadowed by the curtains I won't open today –
you tell me how you hated to see me snooze
in another's arms this year:

(handwritten: jealous lover)

my eyes shining like candles on a birthday cake,
my tongue dumb as a baby mouse, my hair
a dollop of syrup.
My body has been loose and happy. I'm getting a belly,
laughing at utter trivialities –
not your girl.

(handwritten: personifying the depression)

Where did that pale face that haunted you so
go? Where's the knife-drawer of her ribs?
Is she blind now to bleeding?
Why won't she moan?

You're like an ex I can't shake,
tall, with your impossible drowning eyes,
you take me out for a drink, sink
me into a kiss, play our old tunes, say: 'lie back,
you know you want to,
we belong together…'

(handwritten: descends willingly back into old habits)

and the next thing my kitchen roars with darker weather
and I'm filthy and I'm
fucked.

(handwritten: strong shocking)

(handwritten: easy to give in familiar)

35

To Christchurch

O Christchurch,
your stern brow and fingerbone steeple,
beckon me home, as I stumble back, heeled
and dizzy with drink.
Pale spearhead –
rats' skull!

You have stared, dead-eyed,
on so much weeping and winning,
such fucking and sinning –
the Ripper's dissections
and Rosenberg's face
lifting to you a last time...

O you are vile and beautiful –
turning the colour of curds in the morning light,
or blue-skinned at the edges of night –
Beaked monster!
White whale!

I have loved you so long,
and it explained it as grace
or your porcelain face,
but you are the colour of the coldest sweat –
what we try to forget –
and I always knew what you meant.

To a Pigeon

So there you are, each day, pecking the street
   for – what? Some dirt or necessary grit?
The maw of a kebab too hot to eat?
   A hooker's condom, or your own loose shit?
A petal of skin sloughed from my own face?
   Not that – hungover –my own diet is good,
      I pass you – and those girls out on the game –
      for crisps, pop, pain erased,
fingers clownish; muffled with zinging blood,
and cannot help but feel we are same.

Pigeon, you see I drink from any cups
   to turn these visions' voices down to low –
and now my hair's a rat's pelt, my nose drips,
   whilst your feathers are dingy, the rainbow
hooping your neck is like the oil on soup.
   We neither of us, pigeon, look our best!
      Yet still you scrabble on this concrete stretch –
      how easily we stoop,
and lose our better selves when put to test,
by ugliness, and lack, my fellow wretch!

Pigeon, I know that we should count our luck.
   You're the same bird swooped over the darkest mills,
when Dickens walked, and children died in muck,
   before this age of TV, pizza, pills,
and rich pickings for you in wasteful bins –
   but still some louse infects my sullied mind,
      and so I am surprised when I, like you
      for all my selfish sins
can stand here nourished by this world I find:
these autumn leaves like lamps against the blue.

Yes you are like the matted fox that paws
   bags for korma behind the curry house;
you're like the children, sprinting to the doors
   of tourist buses deep in calloused Laos
and sucking protein gleefully from cheap
   boiled eggs heavy and boned with lifeless chicks.

Yes – parasite – though this world often seems
        so absurd I can't weep,
too nauseated by gameshows and dicks,
and hope that thins, and falters to bad dreams –

I dwell on you, and feed despite the dirt,
    and there's a courage lies in that, I think.
The cherry blossom, with its thousand skirts
    might be enough to float me, when I sink,
a kiss might be enough – like the cherry
        tumbled from market stall that you now eat –
            to sweeten things, when death's breath heats my throat.
                Winged Sisyphus! Very
glad is my soul, when I see your wings beat
up tower-block high, and cross Heaven's blue moat

To Absinthe

A sugar cube flickers on the slatted spoon –
a bubbling milk tooth – drips into fennel green,
the glut of booze to glaze the world, to gloze
and gloss over these stalking mares,
the hard facts of cell and scared.
You – green fairy – leave stenching breath
under pillows in exchange for
a few hours of a life,
a slither of ear.

Lift me out of compassion and passion!
Wipe me good and blank like bleach on a stain,
like anaesthetic
on pain.

To a London Plane Tree

Your bark flakes rose, cream and stone –
the walls in a bedsit painted one time too many –
and seedpods dangle from your branches:
necklaces found on an archaeological dig.
You are as big as a church.

Centuries ago they planted you,
knowing you'd withstand the filth and smog.
Me, I'm just passing on my way back from work.
It's 6.30, and the hood of my anorak
slips off as I stare up into your tallness.

O Plane tree!
I must seem a bead of wet in the mist,
a mote of the dirt you endure.
I am a point of light in a Catherine Wheel,
and you are the pin.

III

Home

The Beginning of the End

Will I say that it began that day last week –
when I was back from travelling, in my new flat,
surrounded by flat-packs and boxes of books,
on the third day of the heatwave?

Recount how I cut through a peach with a knife –
furred like the skin of a forearm, yolk gold, stone –
and worried, because I was late by a week,
and felt, in my nervy, uncertain state,

blessed by the kindness of people –
how warmly they had welcomed me home
(Nicky bringing a glass of wine as I changed in her bathroom,
Helen with her box of things: can opener, loo roll, chickpeas)?

Will I recall how, hunching in a cling of sweat,
I tried to press words against my pages –
as I tried to bang the plague of fruit flies, bred in the swelter,
flat against my wall – but instead, distracted

turned to the papers, the nervy headlines:
Global Warming: Is it Upon Us?
The Heat is On,
Global Warning,

then waded into town where the shops shivered
with air-conditioning, and people packed supermarket bags
with extra cans of beer, pre-washed salad leaves,
disposable barbecues, shrink-wrapped peaches?

Will I say that it began that day last week –
my knowledge, that it was happening, actually, now?
Will I say: after that it happened so quickly –
the floods, the skies of liver and indigo,

the rationing of water, malaria, tsetse flies;
that soon no one would come back from a trip around the world –
not the same world anyway – tanned
and talking of Australia (a wasteland now, uninhabitable?)

Will I speak of that day in a house
with the blinds all shut, hunched beside a radio –
listening to a litany of lost things: certain Pacific islands,
the iris sofarana of Lebanon, red deer...?

Will no one wobble upstairs with glasses of white wine
to a room where a girl puts on lipstick?
Or make their son and his girlfriend a box of essentials
that includes plum tomatoes but not sunblock?

Will my words mean nothing, with no one to read them
(and people only ever heard the words they wanted anyway)?
Will I be gladder than ever that two days later
after finally purchasing a pregnancy test, I bled?

Or no. None of that. Will it all carry on
as it always does, and I'll cut peaches for my children,
eat peaches and tut at the hysteria of headlines?
Yes, please god, lets cling to that –

or is that the beginning?

The Chain

I am pale as tequila,
in black, and my skirts made of smoke,
I smile at your joke,

give you change to feed to machines
that flicker like adverts in puddles,
like terrible dreams.

Ice?
Do you think that I'm nice?
Perhaps I'm just cheap,

minimum wage, yet you all get this show,
get to patronise, blow me a kiss.
Crisp?

I'm your optic illusion.
Less face it, I'm better than real –
walk into a place like this,

any time, it's the same place:
same girl with a different face,
framed posters of postery things,

and the carpets,
the *carpets* –
inspired by the crash

of a tray full of office girl drinks:
shooters and bitch fizz,
liquid kids' TV,

and the music,
the *music*,
that's sweeter and safer than shandy.

The menu you know:
wraps, bangers, combo.
Mayo?

It's been a long day, yes?
Sit down and talk —
I've plenty of empties to stack.

Don't worry, you've no need to listen back.
Wife selfish? Job poo?
Poor darling, poor You.

I cut up raggedly lemons,
like combs jammed full with blonde hair,
whilst you outline the things you deserve...

'What does it take around here to get served?'
Slice? Ice?
The other staff live in a squat,

what with not being paid the price
of a whisky and Coke in an hour.
What did you call me then? *Flower?*

How kind, when I hum of the booze,
a fug I can't lose
even with all that chill walk home

past the taxis and dark spots and *darlings,*
trailing a veil of men's breath,
my hands tacky with froth,

my hair like that splash of Sauvignon Blanc
I tip down the sink at the end.
You think I'm your friend?

In this nowhere you come with your cash,
I clean up the ash.
You think this is real?

Nothing I show you I feel.
That's a small? Extra-Cold? And with glass?
Special Meal Deal?

The Bad News

This evening the sickle of the wind felled a city.
This evening girls slid like new calves to the sand,
eyes webs for flies, tongues thick with thirst's flavour.
This evening ancient vessels went jag-toothed dancing
at the knotty feet of looters, whilst women bayed
like wolves to the star in the power cut's dark,
for their youngest, slain by lion-faced men.

This evening, in dark intestines, super bugs
invisibly bred, knitting their message: death, death.
This evening parents pampered their dolled, rouged tots,
and mothers-of-ten sewed themselves to death,
fumble-fingered on mandatory double-shifts.
This evening a whale's gorgeous callused heft
thrashed the harpoon gut-deep, to rot and nothing.

This evening, the children of Africa kinged and scrapped
amongst the ghostly stones of our outdated fridges.
This evening warheads point their noses at us,
like the fragile, curious noses of wet rats,
and men feasted on the belly of a peacekeeper
in groin-damp jungle where the monkeys cry: *oo oo*.
This evening no one cared what we thought.

This evening a man turned the key of his ignition
and drove 'For the hell of it' through golden hits and suburbs,
and a sea of glass mingled with oil and fire
and seals basked in ineradicable darkness.
This evening politicians plotted profitable slaughter.
This evening a man on a bus opened the gates
to a hundred black horses with manes of flame.

This evening as we waited in the ward for the bad news,
in its faint tang of shit, beside the old man who rocked
and cried out moistly for his 'Mam',
a black alphabet of swallows clouded the low sun,
except I thought that they spelt: death, death,
and I thought that I could hear the whole ill earth tick
closer now, towards the end, into evening.

Notes to Self

1 *Note on the Value of Crap*

That train to my parents' house
ran on its rails like a shudder down a spine,
and it was hard to stare out of the pawed glass
at the ash sky and the fox, that red Anubis,
the bowed heads of buddleia,
the terrible tangle of hawthorn,
the graves flickering like dead screens in the drizzle.
It was easier to gaze down, at thick, shiny paper,
at the diets of stars, the spas, the best ever pesto,
the Truth about some Botox-bloated blonde.
It is almost miraculous, the scope and depth
of our mutual fantasy of champagne and shops;
the fragile paper tower of pretend –
and it was knowing that this season sugar pink is in for nails
that kept me walking up the platform, to that arch
like the mouth of some terrible monster,
still thinking: *I can do this, I can do this.*
I hadn't cried yet, you see.

2 *Note on Self-Pity*

Here I am, rattling around my new flat,
taking unnecessary trips across the plain wooden floors
past the picture you've been saying you'll put up
except shit keeps happening.
On the phone, when she told me,
my mother's voice turned lean and feral:
'Your sister doesn't know shit happens,
but *I* know shit happens.'
I have watered the rosemary bush.
The fennel's dead:
its pale spindles are the skeletons of birds.
I am wearing a cream jumper.

47

I have made myself milky drinks, and now
I am spooning myself soup as to an invalid:
come on, Clare. There, there.
That's it, good girl.

3 Note on Perspective

I thought I was learning perspective,
at the stilt village, with its slippery calves' legs,
the men pulling in their sparse catch:
that patchwork of cages retching muscled, olive fish,
and the mud-jacks heaving themselves through the wet,
and sun plunging, regardless.
A sea eagle stabbed at the reddening heave
then glided on the call to mosque that wept across the waters,
that voice that yearns for what it cannot have,
as so many birds dragged overhead towards the night.
Life, I told myself, grandly,
but look at perspective now:
in the kitchen, beside the bread-bin,
beside the kettle's mean face,
it's all shot, and mum's weeping, and my father upstairs
has the wrong blood count –
such a tiny thing, really, but still.
She starts trying to do the crossword,
and I am gabbling on, like I do, and my gabbling
is all there is between this kitchen and hell.

4 Note on the Scab

So you did it again, stumbling round mussed,
a mess of mouth and easy legs, addled,
the streetlights gold as tens of beery pints,
the cars honking like angry geese,
just hoping that strangers will be cool,
filling the air with sour little grunty calls
to your boy saying *find me, I'm nowhere.*

And wasn't it funny! You really are
alive, really something – it's like the time
you managed not to spill a drop of wine,
when you fell, exactly, like a felled elm,
or the time you fell on the phone to him –
a cry, a thud, the phone-line dead –
and he thought that you'd been mugged.
You crazy thing! Wild card! Muse!
This time you scabbed your knee. It's huge,
and almost black, crisp, like something burnt.
You can't keep your fingers off it.
That botch of blood. Your father's cells
webbing it. Your mother's tough as jewels as well.
It distracts you at work. Beneath the desk it rages.
Your fingers hum against it, the little ridges,
like the ridges on a model of the human brain.
You know you'll make it bleed again.
You'd like a fucking drink right now. Instead
you pick it clean off, like the top of your head.

5 *Note on Love*

My mother says what makes her cry the most
is not the horror, but the magnificence –
the magnificence of so much love,
Tom hoovering and Penny saying she'll buy
a balloon ride for him, if he gets a bit better.
The card with all those scribbled kid's names.
When she lies by my dad on the bed, TV on,
they fit, like the right crossword answers.
What makes me cry the most is how we lie
on the couch, and my head against Rich's chest
makes me think of my father. His jumpers.
It *is* magnificent, to live amidst such love.
This moment. The sparrow. The floor. Pasta.
In hospital I count tears back.
I mutter this charm:
I have you, I have you, I have you.

The Cancer-Dream

At night now, no one is safe –
no excuse made for youth,
or five pieces of fruit,
each dream brings new death:
that shapeshifter coming
for forearm or throat.
An omnivorous goat,
it chews my friend's tit,
then lays fat gull's eggs,
laps my knees like a senile mutt.
It's the slick on the sea,
a promiscuous slut.
I wake up in the night,
and I perch on the loo,
squeezing my bladder tight
(like that's why I woke up!)
and the bulb drips wobbly
dark cells on my eyes,
and Love too seems a cancer,
though cruelly disguised.
It helplessly doubles what's wrong.
It breaks,
        breaks your heart
when it needs to be strong.

October

And after everything, it's now.
The fields are heather-dark with rain,
trampled to bog by all those hooves,
or beds for milk-cool, kneeling cows.
I put out bottles by the bins.
Smoke rises over village roofs.

Scissors drop from the sycamore,
the arms of ash trees shiver bare.
I stare across at Winter Hill,
whilst the crows circle me and caw
and after everything, I'm here,
taking in lungfuls of the chill.

Born twenty-five years ago,
I made it, though a hard breech birth,
and my father ran up this road
to yell up to that stone window
that I was breathing on this earth.
I'm told his joy made him half-mad,

and now he sits upstairs and sees
the moon squat in his window frame,
the wind that shoulders at his gate,
the jay that feeds upon their seeds,
the green of fields he cannot climb,
the fat, pale pear he will not eat.

And after everything, it's now –
the harvest's in, and soon the ghosts
arrive, child-sized, and stalk estates,
and ice makes the grey stream run slow,
and late blackberries spoil in frost.
I'm making tea. I get out plates,

just a small plate now for my dad.
A squirrel quivers on the wall,
this moment sprung in him like fear.
The fireplace burns a homely red,
and I squeeze his hand with my all,
for after everything, I'm here.

Blossom in November

Because I might have sunk beneath this –
a sky the bloodless green of our wall's damp,
and the washing-up slopping in bleary brown water.
My sprained, swaddled wrist. The results from the test.
I might once have reached for that poem –

O my God what am I
That these late mouths should cry open

                                        – and sunk,
and not have tasted the soup that you left me for lunch,
with the lentils like beads,
with the aubergine gone gold to spice,

or looked up from the bowl and felt my heart lift,
in spite of itself, at this fearful gift
of blossom, *now* of all times,
and my ring on the sill by the sink,
and the thought of you driving towards me,
picking me up for that trip down rivers of light
to that hospital car park, and pain, and to face it together,

to drive into our future together.

For My Fiancé

At first, engaged, unused to jewellery,
I turn the ring like a loose tooth –
lying in bed aware of its touch, like the touch
of a finger to thigh. Eyes open to the silvered blinds,
I imagine outside: how the lakes will spangle
and bloat, skies clear and then pummel with storms, rivers
break banks, how roses will explode then gulp
to dust, and towers jerk up
like fingers, counting.
Throughout all this we will wake up together –
crumple-faced, eyes pearled with sleep, grouchy
or thirsting for tea or juice, or you will finger
these breasts until they raise up pips,
stir me where I blizzard and yolk,
make a bead of me;
have me call this pillow to a sour mash.
You will squash me against you when I'm crying like the rain,
croon and comfort. And for you I'll do the same.
Whilst the world wars, darling, such things will stay certain –
these fingers that thread your woolly chest,
this jumble of legs, this nest,
this waking to light and ourselves.

For the Other Ones

Not knowing how the world has forked –
those paths our other selves have walked –
I think now, how you might read this,
like me, uncertain what we missed
with all the choices that we took:
my head is in your lap now, look –

the weight of it. My hair a mess
of blonde you puzzle, as I press
your mouth into my mouth again.
If in this life there's ever pain
then listen carefully. Where we've gone
I whisper: *my beloved one.*

For My Future Daughter

Try not to think too deeply,
try not to think too well.
Heaven is in small details,
labyrinths lead to hell.

Take comfort from the squirrel,
take comfort from the moon –
like a hot buttered crumpet,
a kind face in your room.

And if you are now older
take comfort in his smell,
the fact he's cooked you dinner,
the fact he treats you well.

Try not to think too deeply.
You never can be good.
You'll never find a home that
is not marked with some blood.

And sorry that I brought you
to a world where that's true.
The Protestants hate Catholics.
The Arabs hate the Jews,

and half the world hates you, dear.
But I loved your warm head
before I'd even planned you.
I pictured you in bed

and kissed that absent soft-spot,
and though I am not there,
shut your eyes, squeeze my hand tight,
and though I won't be there

in some way I'll be there, dear.
That is how we persist.
My sweet thing, do forgive me
for selfishness. I kiss

you wherever you are now
and hope you're glad of life –
despite the violent weather
despite the sudden knife –

and that you love that one gift,
that rare thrill of *I am*
as death pans out around you.
Hope that you do not damn

this mother who loved life so,
she hoped she'd live within
you, after: ball your fist, dear,
and feel your nails dig in.

Cordelia at the Service Stop

And you needed the loo, so here I am – mazed by celeb mags,
the grab-bags of crisps. Tepid coffee suds
fill a cup like insulating foam.

My father used to (*used* to) buy me magazines to cheer me up,
but reading in the car makes me throw up,
and the papers' headlines stormcloud my fingers,
and are wrong.

Escalators glide softly
like hospital trolleys.

'Are you okay?' you ask, on your return. My eyes burn.
No sleep and then this monstrous lack of tears

and it's such a stupid question but I cannot heave
my heart
into my mouth, I cannot

heave it

Metamorphoses

Beneath a chicken-blood moon,
high grass trembles – a lip before tears –
and a man's teeth turn flick-knives, and icicle out,
and fur forests the fingers, the scar.

Elsewhere, a man finds he's an insect:
scribble-legs, sunglassy eyes,
a drudge for the morsel, the hive –
and a woman awakens, alive, but made out of glass:

her torso a tank full of awful salmon,
her throat like a flute for champagne,
that could snap with one tap.
Ting!

Orpheus, all lost, transformed
to a tree cloaked in darkest needles,
and Maoris know glaciers of turquoise light,
are the *Tears of the Avalanche Girl,*

so the girl who is spat upon hugs at her knees
and tucks in the head, and is stone.
A true story. *Truly,* the world seems to seek
to make us inhuman, like It.

It hopes we'll freeze over or pine.
Oh, the grief wants to steal the warmth from our bones –
run now, *run,* mother, sister! Do not
let this monster make us its own.

My Father and the Snow

It is a year ago, and I am in Beijing,

in a hostel where kids chow down pot noodles and shoot pool,
away from the stone monkeys and teapots and indifferent freeways,
tap-tapping an email to my parents –
it's New Year, and last night our street
was jumpy with illicit firecrackers,
I type – knowing that my father loves fireworks,
as he loves balconies and the films of Bruce Lee,
as he loves the snow.
Love you, I sign off,
before heading to the Summer Palace with Rich,
pausing to purchase jiaozi in their glass skins,
crinkled like new kittens.

The lake is frozen solid –
a bowl of milk laid out for some great cat,
and the tour guides say: *Empress Dowager Cixi* this and that,
encourage the groups to imagine her stepping out –
as we do onto ice –
                    into her pleasure boat,
(although around us new China is weakening the surface with
            high-heels,
skating in its Sunday best, swigging *Sprites*).

We move out together, the dragon empress and I –
onto the glass, creaking with its wrinkles,
and beneath, the blackness that would make you forget your feet
in moments:
                    a squirming darkness of eels.
She endures in the way I imagine her
posed beside the ornamental duck, the lotus, the lily,
the marble boat she bought to spite the navy,
whilst the heaving, infinite mass of others
lie anonymous beneath solid blank
always.

My father is alive in the world.
I imagine the heat of his breath.

He sleeps now at the other edge of the earth –
how absurd, to think how people curl and cling
to the globe's underside, like rock-pool creatures.

His arm will be around my mum, the TV they left on
going through its bleary, sea-coloured motions,
and I want to show him this scene,
to say: *look I'm in China!*
                    Actual China!
Look at this blinding of white!

*

It is twenty years ago, and I am home,

where New Year is a buffet of curried eggs and vol-au-vents,
then my sister and me carried across the road
from strange beds to our own – fuzzy and cradled –
through that eerie stopped world of cat's stares and lamp glow
on our nighties and naked toes.

The next day my father takes us sledging, putting on
his college scarf, black mac. Wellies. Curls
cupping his handsome, lean face.
My cheeks ring with coldness. My nose
babbles with snot...
                    Then I am sat in position –
'Don't worry, I'll hold onto you' –
and the snow could cover any terror, knoll or rock,
but still we launch towards the reservoir, that basinful of sky,
slithering, and whoosh – I
plunge into it,
                    bundled by his arms.

Another go we chant,
until lamps ping on along the horizon,
and snow starts to twinkle with dark blue eyes.

*

It is now, and I am home.

This New Year's Eve my father's dead.
The path is the pale of a graze, and the church bell
throbs like ice against a bad tooth.
I imagine the heat of his breath.
I can't sob or I would never stop –
though one tear does creep and cling to my cheek:
like a tender maggot or some quiet leech.
Love you, I signed off.

At the wake there are so many stories –
how my dad liked the horses and banana milkshakes,
or made them watch the fight scenes from *Zulu* –
and he endures, I guess, in that, but not enough,
and so I drink too much.
                   I drink to forget
him in the wheelchair at hospital, his optimism,
how he wept as I boarded the train to go travelling,
a year ago. To go to Beijing.
Oh god is there never enough time, enough holding, enough
        I love you, enough?

Wine? Yes, more wine.
There is never enough wine,
each sip's small avalanche numbing my heart.
The bathroom buzzes. I glaze and slur,
and then, at almost midnight, it begins to snow.
Proper big fat flakes! Such beautiful flakes!

And I am out in the yard beneath security light shouting:
       it's fucking snowing, it's fucking snowing –
I mean tonight of all nights! New Year's Eve,
when we've burnt him (that coffin so small, I can't.)

And I start blubbing, suddenly, my little chin wobbling, raw –
a snotty thaw of grief –
and no I can't recall who lifted me up from my knees in the wet,
       but my face
was pulled up to face the tumbling white, and I think it was my father
wiped my eyes and said: 'Don't cry, Clare.

Look, Clare! Look! The snow!'